NORWAY THEN CANADA - A NEW STRATEGY TO AVOID A BREXIT SMASH

By George Trefgarne

"The purpose of democratic statecraft is, or should be, to find the means of ordered liberty in a world condemned to everlasting change."

Arthur M. Schlesinger, Jr. The Cycles of American History

Preface

At the time of writing, Britain is on the verge of a political and economic crisis as our political leaders seem incapable of handling Brexit in a robust manner which commands widespread confidence. The public is fed up with these political games. This paper is motivated by one simple desire. To find a solution to Brexit which works and would be acceptable to the majority of the country, so that we can come together and move on to a prosperous future. For that reason, I dismiss out of hand all politically and economically risky options, such as the disruption of No Deal, or a second referendum, or extending Article 50.

My personal, somewhat uncritical, preference was originally for "Canada Plus, Plus" free trade agreement with the EU. But all of us, including those like me who voted Leave, have to recognise where we are now: in a jam. The Prime Minister, Theresa May, has negotiated poorly and having lost her majority, she faces constant Parliamentary opposition and unhelpfulness from her own side.

I would also like to make clear that falling back on our membership of the European Economic Area Agreement (EEA) is not an original idea of mine and I am a late convert. Like many others, I initially believed assertions by the Government and others that the EEA+EFTA is not a legally possible Brexit option and is anyway incompatible with the EU referendum result, not realising, for instance, that we remain a contracting party and that the EEA includes a right of veto over new legislation and opt outs from freedom of movement.

In particular, I owe thanks to Lord Owen, a former Foreign Secretary, for writing the Forward to this paper, and to Prof. George Yarrow, Rupert Darwall and Nick Boles MP. I have also relied on existing material published by Civitas, Briefings for Brexit and the Institute for Government, among others. I also note that lonely voices, such as the journalist Christopher Booker, have advocated the Norway option all along.

My unique contribution is to dust off my skills as a former Economics Editor of the Daily Telegraph and the owner of a PR firm to bring the idea together and to help project it. I have done so, simply because I believe it is the right thing to do. For evil to triumph, it is only necessary for good people to sit back and do nothing. Although I was not personally actively involved in the referendum campaign, I hope I have been able to get a good hearing on all sides.

Foreword

This paper is an excellent explanation of a complex, serious and important Brexit option that urgently faces Parliament on a cross party basis. The urgency stems from President Macron's totally predictable decision on 27 August 2018, as the EU's most powerful federalist, to reject the scheme which emerged from the Chequers meeting in July 2018.

A unilateral United Kingdom decision on continued membership of the European Economic Area Agreement, given the nature of Article 50, is the only rational option and it should be put into legislative form by a cross party motion supported by as many MPs as possible. The Government should be clear with Parliament and the public that this is a legal option which remains available to the United Kingdom. We remain a contracting party to the EEA and the Treaty can be made fully operative without too much difficulty.

The legislation should be simple and focused and state only that the U.K. will remain within the European Economic Area Agreement as a non-EU member until Parliament decides otherwise. It would act as an instruction to the government.

The government should then discuss the legislative decision with the three non-EU signatories to the European Economic Area Agreement – Norway, Iceland and Lichtenstein - and with the 28 other EU signatories, including the European Commission, once this legislative authority has been voted on by the House of Commons. Only after the size of the cross party support is assessed will it be possible to clarify with the other EEA parties exactly how it can be given effect to making the Treaty operative, when Article 50 lapses on 31 March 2019.

The British government can of course indicate its intention in relation to giving the statutory one year's notice for leaving the EEAA at any point in this process.

I would personally argue that a commitment to give such a year's notice of an intention to leave should be given sometime during the lifetime of this Parliament before May 2022.

The Rt Hon Lord David Owen, FRCP, CH.

Norway then Canada

1. The problem

On current trajectory, the UK is heading towards a Brexit smash.

The two choices effectively on offer are either a deal on the EU's terms as initiated at Chequers in June, unacceptable to Remainers and Leavers alike, or a No Deal scenario. The latter is tempting for some Brexiteers, as they have an extravagant faith in the World Trade Organisation's rules and they believe the threat of No Deal would hasten both the UK and the EU into signing a Canada Plus Free Trade Agreement (FTA).

While there may be elements of the Chequers proposals which are attractive, the combination of a common rule book, a common customs area and EU influence over UK social and environmental legislation, all adjudicated by tribunals presumably looking up to the European Court of Justice, make it an abrogation rather than an expression of sovereignty. And the EU does not like its "cherry-picking" approach. There was also something underhand and depressing in the way the Prime Minister inflicted it on the Cabinet, going behind the backs of minister is the Department for Exiting the European Union (DEXEU).

The Brexiteers – gathered around the 60-odd members of the European Research Group in Parliament - are honourable men and women, but they have seriously miscalculated or been trapped, depending on your point of view. There is no majority in the Cabinet, Parliament, or the country for the short-term economic disruption and risk which would accompany the No Deal alternative to Chequers that they advocate. As a recent article in the Sunday Times illuminated, the Government's No Deal preparations are a PR disaster, with talk of food and medicine shortages[1].

To work successfully, No Deal or WTO rules would require numerous minor agreements with the EU on mutual recognition, air travel, certification,

---

[1] The Sunday Times. Don't panic, we will deal with No Deal! 29th July 2018.

regulatory, food and sanitary compliance which are not in place. Hence the use by some of the *non sequitur* "a No Deal deal".

Furthermore, even if there was widespread public support for No Deal, the hiatus would hand yet more leverage to the EU which would extract its pound of flesh in return for acquiescence in the Canada Plus agreement advocated by Brexiteers. The EU's motives are, in the short term, 'imperial' and not merely economic. The EU is perfectly entitled to assert its sovereign political interest, just as we are entitled to assert ours.

The miscalculation of the Brexiteers is matched on the other side of the argument by those agitating for a second referendum, the so-called People's Vote. Surreptitiously, this is also premised on there being No Deal, but to be followed by a delay in the UK's departure from the EU[2]. Another referendum might appear superficially attractive to some, but by the time the legislation is passed, the question(s) agreed, the rules updated, the campaigns designated and referendum conducted, at least two years would have passed. What would happen in the meantime? And how would the public react to being asked to vote again? This is another potentially disastrous option to be avoided.

The UK economy is already growing below trend; business investment is flatlining, further diminishing the outlook for productivity; consumer confidence remains depressed; and households are borrowing to prop up their incomes because the consequent weakness of sterling has driven down real earnings[3]. The Bank of England is raising interest rates. We risk once again becoming the sick man of Europe.

Rather than accept No Deal and faced with the short-term economic consequences, Parliament will likely press for a humiliating climb down, perhaps

---

[2] The game on this was given away in a piece in The Times by Matthew Parris, who is in favour of reversing the referendum, entitled Here is to the success of the Brexit headbangers, 25th August 2018.

[3] CapX. It is official, Brexit uncertainty is hitting the economy.

through triggering the delay of Exit Day using the provisions of S.20 (4)[4] of the EU Withdrawal Act or the "Humble Address" procedure (which the Opposition can use to compel the Government to do something via a vote in the House of Commons). For its part, the European Council can extend Article 50, with the agreement of the member state concerned using section (3) of that provision.

There are numerous legal devices which the majority of MPs can use to force a vote on a No Deal Brexit, and to stop it. We should assume that will happen.

The political consequences for the Government and the country of a delayed and bungled Brexit would be dire. The economic costs of such prolonged uncertainty could also be severe.

How do we get out of this mess?

2. The solution: Norway for now

There is a way out, hiding in plain sight. An off-the-shelf Plan B which already works.

The UK should abandon the current strategy, by dropping or substantially revising the existing proposed Withdrawal Agreement with its penal and complex Implementation Period and instead adopt a new two stage approach.

First, fall back on membership of the European Economic Area and the related European Free Trade Association (EFTA). This is known as "the Norway option".

Second, use that as a platform to negotiate a new relationship with the EU, such as a proper Canada Plus arrangement.

---

[4] EU Withdrawal Act Section 20 (4) states: "A Minister of the Crown may by regulations amend the definition of "exit day" …to ensure that the day and time specified in the definition are the day and time that the Treaties are to cease to apply to the United Kingdom".

This new strategy was first suggested by Prof. George Yarrow of both Oxford University and the Regulatory Policy Institute (RPI) and has since been taken up by a variety of influential figures. I recommend George Yarrow's papers on the RPI and Briefings for Brexit websites. He is really the intellectual father of this strategy.

Why? Principally because the Norway option works and it would restore what has been so foolishly discarded by Theresa May – negotiating leverage, optionality and certainty. The recovery in UK political and economic confidence could be dramatic. This a prize sensible people on all sides of the debate should fight for.

3. The EEA's advantages

The EEA was signed in Porto in May 1992 by the EU, individual member states in their own right, and the members of EFTA. It was ratified and brought onto the UK statute book via the European Economic Area Act 1993[5].

It is a commercial Treaty which, according to Article 1, is intended to "promote a continuing and balanced strengthening of trade and economic relation."[6] It delivers Brexit and is superior to the Implementation / Transition Deal because it includes rights as well as obligations. It enables participation in the single market, facilitates trade and co-operation with the EU, but is outside the EU. There is no mention of "ever closer union" or common citizenship. The EFTA participating members are Norway, Lichtenstein and Iceland. Switzerland is also a member of EFTA, but not the EEA.

The EEA has numerous advantages, making it on any rational basis superior to No Deal on WTO terms, the Implementation Period and the Chequers proposals:

---

[5] European Economic Area Act 1993.

[6] European Economic Area Treaty, Article 1

- We are already a contracting party in our own right, limiting the EU's ability to object

- It is a functioning free trade agreement with the EU

- It would return the UK to the position it is most comfortable with in its relationship with the EU, a common market based on a commercial Treaty agreed between sovereign nations

- The City would retain its passporting rights for financial services

- It is outside the Customs Union, so we would be free to sign trade deals

- There would be no money to pay on day one and the £40bn exit payment comes off the table

- There are low or zero tariffs on most items traded with the EU except agricultural and food products

- It enables participation in the Single Market but is outside the jurisdiction of the European Court of Justice, the Common Agricultural Policy and Common Fisheries Policy

- It has established, working institutions and processes, including the opportunity to shape, adapt or even veto new legislation

- It allows for opt outs, limits and safeguards to freedom of movement of workers

- There is no common citizenship and British passports would be restored

- It removes the necessity for the so-called Irish Backstop

- It would restore optionality to our relationship with the EU, so we could negotiate a proper Canada Plus agreement

4. How the EEA works

In the EEA, contracting parties are members of one of two governance pillars: the European Union one (as is currently the case for the UK), or the EFTA one. For the Treaty to operate after the UK leaves the EU, the UK must join the EFTA pillar.

The entire EEA system, as practised by the EFTA pillar, is very different to the EU and is controlled by the nation states.

The EFTA Council is the governing body of EFTA. It meets 8 times a year at ambassadorial level and twice a year at ministerial level. The Council is supported by the EFTA Secretariat, based in Geneva. The chairmanship of the Council rotates between member states every six months.

The relationship between the two pillars is mediated by the various joint bodies, including the EEA Council, which meets at ministerial level twice a year, and the EEA Joint Committee, where ambassadors of the EFTA states meet with EU officials eight times a year.

The decision to incorporate EU single market legislation into the EEA is taken by the EEA Joint Council. However, unlike on the EU side, EFTA states have substantial "adaptation" rights when it comes to implementing the legislation domestically. They also have other legal rights, including, in extremis, a right of "reservation" or veto.

During the drawing up of new single market legislation EFTA member states have the right to be consulted via the "decision shaping process" in Article 99 of the EEA Agreement. The agreement allows for the participation of EFTA experts in the preparatory work of the EU Commission and for participation of EFTA officials on relevant EU Committees.

On the EFTA side, the EFTA Surveillance Authority is responsible for monitoring compliance with agreed rules and the ultimate court is the EFTA Court. Importantly, the EFTA Court does not have the power to direct national courts, only EFTA states. This is another significant difference with the European Court of Justice.

5. The legal position

The legal position of the UK in relation to the EEA and EFTA is critical and potentially confusing. In preparing this note I have taken counsel from numerous eminent lawyers and in doing so, it became apparent that even in that distinguished profession, opinions are coloured by political views. Some hard core Brexiteers and Remainers are united in their view that the strategy outlined in this paper is legally difficult or would be vetoed by the EU. For opposite motives, they view EU law as supreme and ignore the legal reality that the EEA Agreement is a valid Treaty between states governed by the conventions and norms codified in the 1969 Vienna Convention on the Law of Treaties.

The situation is further complicated by the fact that the Government has been contradictory on the subject. A Freedom of Information request to see the Government's legal view has been declined.

The purpose of this paper is not to go into lengthy legal argument. But I am confident that my view is supported by numerous practically minded QCs and lawyers, including Sir Richard Aikens, a former Lord Justice of Appeal. His views are quoted in his own words and at greater length on the Briefings for Brexit website. [7].

I argue that:

- The UK is a contracting party in its own right to the EEA Agreement and remains so until such time as it gives 12 months notice under the Article 127. It has not given such notice and it was conspicuously absent from the so-called Article 50 letter sent by Theresa May in March 2017[8]. Was it left out deliberately by one of the drafters, who foresaw the issue?

---

[7] Briefings for Brexit. The EEA Agreement: the key to a simplified Brexit Process, by Sir Richard Aikens, George Yarrow and Professor Guglielmo Verdirame

[8] Prime Minister's letter to Donald Tusk, 27th March 2017

- There is nothing in the EEA Agreement or the EU Treaties which says withdrawal from one Treaty entails withdrawal from the other.

- The international legal framework which governs the operation of treaties is the Vienna Convention on the Law of Treaties (VCLT). A Treaty remains in force unless it is terminated under its own provisions and there is no basis for termination by implication. It would require a unanimous agreement among the other parties – the 27 EU states, the EU itself and the three EFTA states - to forcibly expel the UK from the EEA.

- However, it is true that once the UK has left the EU, the Treaty will no longer "operate" as far as the UK is concerned. For it to operate, the UK will need to apply to move into the EFTA governance pillar. The repeated use of the expression "the EEA will no longer operate" to suggest we are leaving the EEA simply because we are leaving the EU is a circumlocution, a verbal evasion by the Government which is misleading.

- The European Economic Area Act, 1993, which ratifies the EEA and puts it onto the UK statute has not been repealed.

- In order to make the EEA operable for the UK again it will require the agreement of the members of EFTA on the one hand and the EU and its members on the other and a minor Treaty amendment. But this is a formality.

- The EFTA states have broadly already been receptive.

- The EU has given no indication it would refuse to accommodate the UK staying in the EEA and making it operable by applying to join EFTA. If it did so, or tried to expel the UK from the EEA, or became difficult in some way, the UK could ultimately appeal to the International Court of Justice (ICJ) in the Hague, which arbitrates the VCLT. Our claim would be that the EU or other contracting parties had broken their good faith obligation to make the Treaty work.

- In addition to the VCLT, the legal maxim, applicable in international law *Ut res magis valeat quam pereat* – the thing should be made to work, rather than fail – would apply.

As a political judgement, the UK therefore has significant sovereign legal rights and options under the EEA which we are crazy to discard or fail to assert.

Furthermore, it is extremely unlikely that the EU would wish to have a lengthy, futile and embarrassing legal battle trying to stop the UK asserting its legitimate Treaty rights. Such a course would have existential risks to the organs of the EU as the ICJ could find that the treaties of the EU, which form its constitutional basis, are subject to higher international law. Perhaps US President Donald Trump was right when he advised Theresa May to consider suing the EU and she should not have laughed it off while simultaneously herself negotiating so poorly.[9]

It should also be noted that in February 2017 the High Court dismissed an application by campaigners from an organisation called British Influence for judicial review attempting to show that the Government could only remove Britain from the EEA by legislating to give notice under Article 127 of the agreement was dismissed, but only because the High Court ruled that "the situation has not yet occurred." In its evidence, Government lawyers pleaded that it had not yet decided how it was going to leave the EEA. In other words, it did effectively concede we remain a contracting party and have not yet given notice we are leaving.[10]

How has the Government, in particular the Prime Minister, got into this position? My instinct is that originally falling back on the EEA was dismissed as less flexible than a big, bold free trade deal, along the lines of Canada. There was an exaggerated concern in the Prime Minister's circle that the EEA was not tough enough on freedom of movement. Like many former Remainers, the Prime Minister often seems mistakenly to regard the Brexit vote as mostly about

---

[9] BBC1, interview with Theresa May on the Andrew Marr Show, 15th July 2018.

[10] The Guardian. Fresh Brexit legal challenge blocked by High Court. 3rd February 2017.

cutting immigration, as opposed to a popular expression of a desire for enhanced sovereignty and accountability (of which immigration is only a component).

Whatever the historical explanation, ministers should now familiarise themselves with the true legal position and publish it. The UK has always adhered to its international obligations and it is surprising that the Prime Minister persists at this late stage in attempting to remove the UK from the rights and obligations of an important and valuable Treaty either by subterfuge or by accident, as is apparently happening in the case of the EEA.

6. Growing support

The idea of falling back on the Norway option (if not the second stage of the strategy) was already supported by some commentators and campaigners. But it has recently attracted wider attention, for example:

- The Times. The Norway option is a Brexit plan that could placate both sides. 25.7.2018. By David Smith.

- The Telegraph. Britain's politics have been broken by Brexit, leaving Norway as the only way forward. 23.7.2018. By Jeremy Warner.

- The Telegraph. The Norway option is the only one left which will save Brexit, but Theresa May will have to go first. 18.7.2018. by Philip Johnston.

- Conservative Home. The Conservatives face a choice, seek to park the UK in the EEA under a new Tory leader, or move on. 19.7.2018. By Paul Goodman.

- Evening Standard. Why EFTA may be the only way to save Brexit – Stephen Hammond. 24.07.2018. By Stephen Hammond.

- CAPX. The Norway option can save Brexit. 16.07.2018. By George Trefgarne.

- REACTION. There is a no deal option – it's called the EEA. 16.07.2018. By Rupert Darwall.

- Spectator Coffee House. How the Brexiteers can still save Brexit. 30.07.2018. By Rupert Darwall.

- CAPX. The Norway option is a credible Brexit solution. 02.08.2018. By George Yarrow

- The Sunday Times. Norway's snow crab can lead us to a smooth Brexit which preserves national sovereignty. 05.08.2018. By David Owen.

A grass roots pressure group called EFTA4UK has also been formed which has been tweeting and blogging vigorously. It is also working on creating an All Party Parliamentary Group.

7. The centrality of the Brexiteers

That said, overt support in Parliament for falling back on the EEA is limited and has until recently been led by Stephen Hammond on the Conservative side and Stephen Kinnock, the Labour MP for Aberavon and a prominent Remainer. It has to be conceded that these efforts have thus far not attracted many Brexiteers. But with the founding of a new campaign called Better Brexit by Nick Boles MP, that may change.

This Norway then Canada strategy would only work if it is acceptable to Brexiteers in Parliament and despite some honourable exceptions, like Lord Owen, currently it is not. To be convincing it would also have to be led by a Brexiteer. After all, Brexiteers did win the referendum and they are committed to regaining control of laws, borders and money. Any strategy must also be acceptable to the majority of the 17.2m Brexit voters and their political representatives.

Leaving aside the misunderstanding about whether the UK remains a contracting party to the EEA or not (dealt with above), the issue is that many Brexiteers believe that the EEA option is an unsatisfactory "half-in-half-out" strategy. And they believe this because they hold a number of serious misconceptions. The irony is that many of these myths were originally spread by the Remain side in the Referendum who were keen to polarise the debate. Prior to that, many Brexiteers were in favour of "being like Norway".

8. Addressing the misconceptions about EEA

There are numerous misconceptions about the EEA. These are addressed below.

1. We would have to accept freedom of movement

Wrong. This is the most important misunderstanding, apparently held by the Prime Minister. While freedom of movement of <u>workers</u> is part of the EEA Treaty, there are two opt-outs. The first is under Article 112, which allows any member to take "safeguard measures" to address any "societal or environmental difficulties of a sectorial or regional nature". It is under this section that Lichtenstein has introduced strict limits to immigration since 1997.

The second is Article 28 (3) which allows for freedom of movement "subject to limitations justified on grounds of public policy, public security or public health". It is under this section that Norway has introduced numerous restrictions, such as ID cards for construction and hygiene workers. In principle, the 'public policy' gateway could be used to limit aggregate numbers of work permits.

The UK could unilaterally invoke a Article 112 safeguard to limit immigration and then go through the process to formalise it via a protocol, just as Lichtenstein has done for more than 20 years. This strategy was recently given the approval of the Home Affairs Select Committee of the House of Commons. In a report on post-Brexit immigration policy, it said:

> "Within an EFTA-style arrangement with close or full participation in the single market, we highlight a range of further measures that might be possible - especially in a bespoke negotiated agreement. These include 'emergency brake' provisions, controls on access to the UK labour market,

and further measures which build on the negotiation carried out by the previous Prime Minister. We conclude that there are a series of options for significant immigration reform that should be explored"[11].

2. We would have to carry on paying into the EU Budget

Wrong. The EEA requires no payments into the EU Budget. Instead, members pay (a) agreed contributions for discretionary participation in specific EU agencies and programmes, such as the Erasmus student exchange programme or the Galileo satellite project and (b) 'EFTA grants' made directly (not via the EU) to poorer EU states to support economic and social development. The latter, in reality a form of international aid, are calculated relative to GDP and Professor George Yarrow estimates the total UK contribution would be around £1.5bn, down from a net £9.4bn which the UK paid to the EU in 2016. But much will depend on what EU programmes we wish to continue with.

Norway, which is very wealthy due to its oil and gas industry, makes some discretionary payments called "Norway grants" for reconstruction in former communist states. The UK would be under no obligation to do so, but if it decided to these could arguably come out of the overseas aid budget.

3. We would have to follow all the EU's rules without any say over them

Wrong. We would have to follow the rules, by and large, of the Single Market. But it has been calculated that this is only 28% of total EU laws[12]. Many of these anyway originate in global standards bodies of which the UK is already separately a member.

---

[11] Policy options for future migration from the European Economic Area, Interim Report, by Home Affairs Select Committee, July 2018

[12] The EU Acquis by Richard North on the EU Referendum Blog. He calculates a combined 2,718 EU directives and regulations are in force in the EEA, compared to 9,685 in the EU, or 28%.

The EEA is a flexible, commercial agreement which provides just the sort of rights of consultation and adaptability which would suit the UK as a sovereign, but co-operative trading nation.

Under the EEA Agreement, EFTA members have the right to be consulted on new single market legislation via the so called "decision shaping process."

Norway has some 200 diplomats and experts based in Brussels who participate in the development and drafting of new rules and directives. In effect, they are embedded in the European Commission, which is where most of the de facto power over the detail of economic legislation is located.

Critically, Article 102 of the agreement allows something called "reservation" or a right of veto over rules which a member does not agree with. This is, admittedly, a somewhat nuclear option. But flowing from it is a whole system of co-operation between Norway and the European Commission in rule-making.

If the EU passes a law EFTA does not agree with it can first conduct a relevance assessment, to see if it is covered by the Agreement. For instance, it is on this basis that Norway has ignored various energy and maritime directives.

If that doesn't work Norway can demand "adaptations" to make a new rule suitable. In this way it has changed some 40% of services directives. It can also delay implementation of new rules, and claim it is a derogated matter, better dealt with at state level. A good example is a directive in oil and gas extraction, 90% of which does not apply to Norway after it kicked up a fuss[13].

There is even a provision for developing equivalence of legislation, as opposed to full alignment. Article 102 (4) states: "If.....an agreement on an amendment of an Annex to this Agreement cannot be reached, the EEA Joint Committee shall examine all further possibilities to maintain the good functioning of this Agreement and take any decision necessary to this effect, including the possibility to take notice of the equivalence of legislation."

---

[13] Civitas. The Norway Option. By Jonathan Lindsell

George Yarrow has also drawn attention to the eloquent Norwegian snow crab case. Norway has refused to recognise the right of EU licensed Baltic vessels to fish for these massive, tasty crustaceans in the waters in its continental shelf around the island of Svalbard and has even seized vessels and levied fines. The EU has asked the EFTA Surveillance Authority to take action, but it has refused.

4. The EFTA Court just does as it is told by the ECJ

Wrong. While it is true that the EFTA Court and the ECJ work to create a homogenous approach, the EFTA Court is autonomous. In a 2016 lecture at King's College the former President of the EFTA Court, Dr Carl Baudenbacher[14], made it clear that the EFTA court is not bound to follow the ECJ. He cited 11 cases where the EFTA court had deviated from the ECJ. These included the *Inconsult* case where the EFTA court disagreed with the ECJ and said an insurance company could use an online portal for a contract and did not have to provide a hard copy. In evidence to the DExEU Select Committee Dr Baudenbacher also noted that over 50% of EFTA Court cases were 'new', dealing with issues not previously considered by the ECJ. The EFTA Court therefore very frequently 'went first' and was faster and 'more economic' in its approach than the ECJ.

Separately, Dr Baudenbacher has said he believes the UK could appoint two out of five judges to the EFTA Court[15].

5. We are leaving the EEA anyway once we leave the EU, so it is not possible

Wrong. As outlined in my explanation of the legal position above, the UK is a contracting party in its own right to the Agreement and can only leave if it triggers the exit provision, Article 127, with 12 months notice. The Government

---

[14] Dr Carl Baudenbacher. After Brexit, is the EEA an option for the United Kingdom? Lecture at Kings's College, 13th October 2016.

[15] Reuters. UK could get outsized power if it joins the EFTA Court. 29th November 2017.

has subtly evolved its position on this. Initially, it claimed we would be leaving automatically but this changed around the time of the judicial review application by British Influence in February 2017. In letters to Lord Owen[16], the Prime Minister said in December 2016 that the EEA would "cease to apply" to the UK once we left the EU. However, in February 2018, she changed this to saying it would "no longer operate". This confusing technical position can be easily resolved.

As stated in the legal position above, the EEA has two governance pillars, and the only substantive requirement to make the Agreement operative is that the UK is in one or the other pillar. All the UK needs to do to make the Treaty operative is to apply to join the EFTA pillar and it is very unlikely the other parties would or could withhold consent.

6. Customs services will not be ready

It is possible the relevant customs systems would not be ready for the UK to fall back on the EEA by March 2019. If that is the case, a temporary customs union would have to apply, time limited, perhaps for a few months and no more than a year or two. This is merely an administrative and technical issue and should not be seen as insuperable.

7. We won't be able to negotiate trade deals

Wrong. The EEA is outside the EU Customs Union and its Common Commercial Policy. In general, the EFTA States jointly negotiate free trade deals, as they have in 27 deals with 43 other countries. However, they can negotiate their own bilateral deals, as Switzerland has done, with additional deals with Japan and China. Norway also has its own trade deal with China. Initially, we could join EFTA's existing free trade deals and there would be no need to port across the EU's free trade deals, although these are more comprehensive. The main point is that the UK would have recovered control over its trade

---

[16] Correspondence between Lord Owen and the Prime Minister on the merits of the EEA during the transition period, published on his blog.

policy, enabling the Department for International Trade to sign additional deals around the world.

8. Rules of Origin would create major costs and paperwork for UK firms

Wrong. In the EEA, without a customs union, UK businesses would have to apply Rules of Origin. Where a normal free trade deal (i.e. not a Customs Union) is in play at some stage in a supply chain, in order to benefit from the lower (usually zero) tariff that has been negotiated, exporting companies have to produce a certificate demonstrating that their goods were mostly made where they apparently come from. Given that the hundreds, sometimes thousands of parts in some complex items, like a car or smart phone, come from numerous countries across lengthy supply chains, this can be complicated.

Rules of Origin are therefore operated wherever there is an FTA, and FTAs are ubiquitous in world trade, including EU FTAs with third countries. They affect UK exporters right now, when they export to countries with which the EU has an FTA, e.g. South Korea and Canada. They will affect UK exporters in the event of a future FTA with the USA.

The costs imposed have obviously not been sufficient to seriously hinder the growth of world trade. It is routine and familiar 'paperwork', whose costs are falling as procedures go online. Jonathan Lindsell, who wrote a paper for the think tank Civitas, says that in all the research he did, including interviews with Norwegian businesses, nobody raised Rules of Origin as a problem[17].

A good is deemed to come from where the last "substantial transformation" took place and, as Mr Lindsell notes, this can be an advantage as it might encourage companies to locate more operations in the UK. There is clear evidence for this already. Nissan UK has made significant efforts to organise events for auto component manufacturers worldwide, asking them to consider onshoring new facilities in the UK, possibly in the North East near its Sunderland plant.

---

[17] Civitas. The Norway Option. By Jonathan Lindsell

9. It does not deal with the Irish border issue

Wrong. The EEA removes the necessity for the Paragraph 49 Joint Report promise, the so-called Irish backstop. To remind you that promises that "in the absence of agreed solutions [on the Irish border], the United Kingdom will maintain full alignment with those rules of the Internal Market and the Customs Union". This is a way of saying that unless the UK agrees to no hard border in Ireland, the entire UK will be forced back under the aegis of the EU.

The EEA removes the necessity for Paragraph 49 because we would be in broad alignment on single market rules and, although we would be outside the Customs Union, neither the EU nor the Republic of Ireland (also a contracting party to the EEA) would have legal grounds to object.

The overarching principle of the EEA Treaty is to facilitate trade. This is made clear in Article 1, which says the objective is "is to promote a continuous and balanced strengthening of trade and economic relations between the contracting parties." Not only would the EU itself be in breach by suggesting otherwise, there is clear precedent for it working via bilateral institutions between Norway and other EU members, Sweden and Denmark.

In other words, there would be a border between Northern Ireland and the Irish Republic, but it would be a smooth running and unobtrusive one, perhaps along the lines of Maximum Facilitation partnership originally proposed by David Davis when he was Secretary of State at DEXEU (but blocked by the Prime Minister), underpinned by the working legal structures of the EEA.

10. We will get stuck in EEA and never leave

This, one has to concede, is a potential outcome and one that Brexiteers are concerned about. They smell a rat. But are they right to do so?

In the EEA we would continue to be broadly aligned on Single Market regulation. This is less an issue for goods, but may be a problem for services, where the UK is competitively advantaged and the EU may introduce adverse regulation. A Canada Plus agreement with the EU would provide more independent leeway, but even it has a CETA Joint Committee and an Investor Court System to enforce the provisions of the Treaty. Some sharing sovereignty is inevitable in any system, it is just a question of how much.

One option would be to time limit our participation in the EEA and EFTA, writing into both the Withdrawal Treaty and an Act of Parliament a commitment to leave by, say 2021. However, that also carries risks and should be firmly resisted. There are four reasons why.

> We should have learnt by now that another A50 style deadline would again put the UK over a barrel with the EU and deprive us of negotiating optionality.

> Life is fluid and subject to change. There are two foreseeable scenarios. One is the EEA proves insufficiently flexible and issues emerge with service regulation etc, which mean it would be far preferable to be in a Canada Plus arrangement. In which case the departure from EEA and move to CETA should be back-to-back. The alternative scenario is the EEA does prove flexible enough for our needs and develops in the right way, in which case we won't want to leave. Either way, a fixed date would be folly.

> Just about the only thing which could ruin our negotiations with EFTA is the sense we want to use them as a coaching inn, by giving the impression that the UK wants to turn up and metaphorically put its muddy feet on the beds, then disappear after breakfast without leaving a tip. This is especially important as we will need some goodwill to negotiate the Article112 and Article 28 (3) freedom of movement limits.

In the end it is for politicians and Parliament to decide what trade offs are acceptable and what safeguards or caveats various factions require to make the Norway option palatable. My advice would be to give a political commitment to review the operation of the Norway option after four or five years, to be voted on in Parliament, but to be open minded.

9. Implementation

Implementation of this plan will require six steps which must be executed rapidly and with purpose. They require robust political resolve, energy, and a collaborative approach not just with fellow European states, but across party and between Brexiteers and Remainers. With the right mindset, they should be relatively easy to achieve, given the right political will and leadership.

1. The Government should publish a full and up to date legal assessment, taking account of the views of Sir Richard Aikens and others, confirming that the UK will in fact remain a contracting party to the EEA despite triggering the Article 50 EU exit process and that the UK is also free to ensure the Treaty remains operative by joining the EFTA governance pillar.

2. The UK should notify the EU that it does not intend to sign a Withdrawal Treaty along the lines of the Joint Report and instead negotiate a revised Withdrawal Agreement based on EEA/EFTA membership. We would have to seek the agreement of the EU and the other 27 member states, but for the reasons cited in this paper the likelihood of them withholding it is minimal and we could anyway rely on international legal rights to compel agreement.

3. The UK must apply to join the EFTA governance pillar as soon as possible. In the first instance, this would require applying to join the EFTA Surveillance and Court Agreement. This should be a first step towards seeking full. committed EFTA membership. The decision would be taken unanimously by the EFTA Council on which the four members, Norway, Switzerland, Iceland and Lichtenstein sit.

    A critical part of the negotiations is likely to be the UK admitting an early intention to use both Article 112 and Article 28 (3) of the EEA to control the free movement of workers and the development of a relevant protocol to manage this.

The EEA / EFTA states are apparently eager to welcome the UK. Erna Solberg, the Norwegian Prime Minister, has already suggested she supports the UK falling back on the EEA, telling the Financial Times in May: "I think we will cope very well if the Brits come in. It will give bargaining power on our side too. And it would ease Norway's access to the UK." However, she rightly drew attention to the EEA's "political deficit", it does not have votes in EU institutions[18]. This is what will be most difficult for the UK to accept and why it will not be a long term solution unless that is addressed. Icelandic Foreign Minister Guðlaugur Thór Thórðarson has also said the UK should "definitely join EFTA"[19].

Ms Solberg's comments were echoed more overtly by Thorfinnur Omarsson, spokesman for the EFTA bloc, who reportedly told the website Politico on 26th July 2018: "We are open to receiving a U.K. membership application."[20] EFTA, he said, has not had an indication that this is what London wants yet, but if it takes that option, then the U.K's entry into EFTA "should not be too complicated." However, the decision would be taken unanimously by the four members of the EFTA Council and, despite positive noises from Norway and Switzerland, neither Lichtenstein nor Switzerland have properly indicated how they would vote.

4. It is clear that this Norway option needs the full consent, collaboration and support of Britain's long-standing partner and NATO ally, the Kingdom of Norway. Norway is the biggest and most influential member of EFTA. The arrival of the substantially larger British economy in the institutions of the EFTA governance pillar would fundamentally rebalance it. Furthermore, Norway has legitimate economic interests to consider, in North Sea oil and gas, in its fishing

---

[18] Financial Times. Oslo Thaws on UK joining EEA after Brexit. 13th May 2018.

[19] Interview on BBC Today Programme, 9th May 2017

[20] Politico website, UK drifts towards a Norway style Brexit transition 8th March 2017.

industry and financial services. British ministers and diplomats need to head to Oslo to strengthen and deepen the relationship and to build support as a matter of urgency.

5.   My reading of the UK domestic legal position is that though we will remain contracting parties to the EEA on exit day, it will likely require UK primary legislation for the provisions to continue to operate within the UK under UK domestic law and also to ensure Parliament has approved the application to join EFTA. The explanatory notes which accompanied the EU Withdrawal Bill said:

"The European Economic Area Act 1993 makes the EEA Agreement one of the "EU treaties" for the purposes of the ECA, which implements the EEA Agreement in UK legislation. Therefore, the provisions of the ECA apply to the rights and obligations in the EEA Agreement, so long as the UK is a member of the EU. The EEA Agreement is also implemented domestically through the EEA Act 1993 and other secondary legislation."[21]

6.   One matter which will need resolving delicately is the rights of EU citizens, which were guaranteed (including via justiciability at the ECJ) in the draft Implementation Agreement. This would be replaced by the freedom of movement of workers provision under the EEA, which is equivalent but not identical. The position of UK citizens resident in the EU will also need clarifying.

10. The economic benefits of certainty

What is not commonly appreciated by those on either side of the argument is the economic opportunity cost of Brexit uncertainty, as investors, companies and households hold back on major decisions. Both sides in the debate deserve a share of the responsibility for the opportunity cost, but common sense

---

[21] House of Lords explanatory notes in the Bill Documents for the EU Withdrawal Act.

suggests it is Brexiteers who will ultimately get the blame if an economic crisis ensues.

The impact of uncertainty is especially evident in the inward investment numbers where the OECD has reported a 90% drop in foreign direct inward investment to £15bn in 2017. International investors are eschewing UK equities, leaving companies undervalued and vulnerable to takeovers or activism, and there has been a marked decline in sterling bond issuance. Most tellingly, there has been a noticeable rise in corporate saving. According the Office for National Statistics, corporate deposits and financial balances have risen by 28% since the first quarter of 2015, before the referendum was mooted, to £670bn. House price growth has stalled and both prices and volumes have fallen sharply in London.

Conversely, the prize for creating certainty around Brexit is substantial. Investors would recover their confidence and a tidal wave of delayed or deferred investment in the UK economy would follow. Sterling, and business and consumer confidence, would all recover. The public relief from falling back on the EEA and coming up with a credible solution to Brexit and bringing an end to the negativity and political games in Westminster would be huge.

11. Conclusion

A Brexit political smash would be very dangerous, but that is where we are headed. A sub-optimal Brexit deal, as proposed by the Chequers agreement, would lack political legitimacy and leave the UK handcuffed to the EU with minimal say over its future. A delay to Brexit would undoubtedly fuel a period of profound political controversy and upheaval. No Deal is supposedly still on the table, but the uproar from consumers and business is not something the divided Conservative Party, which has no majority in Parliament, could withstand. We should be confident that Parliament would not allow No Deal to occur and would instead delay Exit Day. But that would not solve anything. Nor would a second referendum.

A political smash would also be nasty. The Conservative party could split and the Government lose a vote of confidence in the House of Commons. A new Government led by Jeremy Corbyn and a sudden General Election might follow. Yet the genius of British political leadership over several centuries has been to avoid such a disastrous *Rex v populi* dispute. Our politicians must not forget their history, or their philosophy.

Brexiteers who are sceptical should accept that life is not perfect. They would be well advised to turn to Lady Thatcher's final book *Statecraft*. In it she wrote:

> "In 1992, Norway Iceland and Liechtenstein – that is the remaining EFTA countries bar Switzerland – concluded negotiations with the EU which established a European Economic Area (EEA). These countries now enjoy free trade with the European Union; that is the freedoms of movement of goods, services, of people and of capital. They also enjoy the unhindered access guaranteed by the operation of the European Single Market. But they remain outside the customs union, the CAP, the CFP, the common foreign and security policy and the rest of the legal/bureaucratic tangle of EU institutions. But Britain is in a different league from countries like Norway (population 4.4 million) or Iceland (population 270,000), let alone Liechtenstein (population thirty-two thousand.) We could press for Britain to be represented in the drawing up of all Single Market Legislation."

She went on:

> "Switzerland is unique in many ways. But whatever Switzerland has secured in its dealings with Europe, Britain too could certainly obtain without great difficulty. Switzerland enjoys free trade with the EU. The EFTA model is perhaps not ideal: but it is certainly an acceptable option."[22]

This is a time for statecraft, for adaptability, for confidence, for vision and for leadership.

---

[22] Statecraft, by Baroness Margaret Thatcher, published by Harper Collins.

It is quite possible that the arrival of the UK as a fully-operative EEA member, as a member of EFTA and participating in its committees and with judges on the EFTA Court, would be utterly transformative for the Association. It could be the beginning of something big, a market oriented, alternative European power base to the EU with global reach and ambition. The economic benefits could also be very substantial.

Yet if we find the Norway option unsuitable in the long term, we can negotiate an alternative free trade agreement from a position of strength. What is to be lost?

If we are to adopt this new, two stage strategy, the UK could escape from the trap it has fallen into. All it requires is political will and leadership. Who among the huddle of Brexiteers has the courage to step forward to seize the opportunity?

Printed in Great Britain
by Amazon